JUST BEARS

JUST BEARS

· SUE QUINN ·

Book Express

Quality and Value in Every Book...

Specially produced for Book Express, Inc,
Airport Business Center, 29 Kripes Road,
East Granby, Connecticut, USA

ISBN 0 86101 500 2

Managing editor: Jilly Glassborow
Editor: Judith Casey
Designer: Glynis Edwards
Photographer: Steve Tanner
Stylist: Sue Duffy
Colour artwork: Malcolm Porter
Typeset by: SX Composing Ltd., England
Colour separation by: Scantrans Pte Ltd., Singapore
Printed by: Proost International Book Production,
Turnhout, Belgium

CONTENTS

INTRODUCTION

*C*apable of evoking the warmest of childhood memories, the teddy bear is one of today's most popular images. Within this charming book you will find bears featured in a wide range of delightful designs, from mirrors and mobiles to sweaters and samplers. And, of course, there is also a traditional jointed teddy bear that will thrill children and adults alike. The designs are made using a variety of popular craft techniques including painting, modelling, wood cutting, knitting, toymaking, appliqué and embroidery, and where necessary we have provided colourful patterns and stitch diagrams for you to follow.

The picture below shows some of the many different materials used to make the designs in this book, including paints, brushes, modelling materials, pieces of wood, fur fabrics, felts, ribbons, balls of wool and embroidery threads. Try to buy good quality materials rather than the cheapest as these will help you to achieve the best results.

To reproduce a pattern to the correct size, first draw up a grid on a piece of paper to the size indicated. Then copy the outline very carefully, one square at a time, on to your grid.

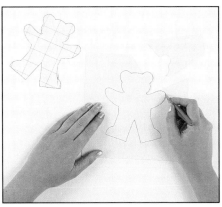

If you need to make your pattern more hardwearing, make a template of the design. Cut out the paper pattern and trace round the outline on to a piece of cardboard. Now cut the template out.

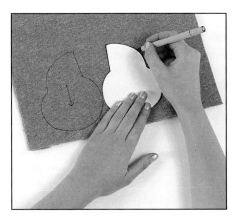

When making soft toys, use your cardboard template to trace the pattern pieces on to fur fabrics. If two asymmetrical pieces are required, turn the template over before tracing the second piece.

Each project is illustrated with a stunning colour photograph and accompanied by detailed instructions showing you how to make it. And, although it would not be possible within the scope of this book to explain all the various techniques involved, there are plenty of hints and tips that will help you achieve the best results.

Many of the projects also feature a scaled down pattern of the design drawn on a grid. The grid is there to help you draw the pattern to the full size using a technique known as 'squaring up' (described below.) The embroidery design, Nursery Sampler, and the knitting pattern, Winter Warmer, are accompanied by charts which you can follow square by square. Each square on the chart represents one stitch.

Squaring Up the Design

On each squared up pattern grid you will find a scale marked, for example: one square represents 2.5cm (1in). Taking a sheet of paper, a felt-tip pen and a long ruler, draw your own grid to the dimensions indicated. Then choose a point on the pattern from which to start. Note which square it occupies and find the corresponding square on your own grid. See where the pattern outline enters and leaves the square and mark these points on your grid. Now join the two points, carefully following the shape of the outline within the square.

Continue to copy the pattern on to your grid square by square and, once you have finished the outline, fill in the details such as the eyes and mouth. Be sure also to mark the direction of pile arrows on each of the toy pattern pieces. This is very important as, if you eventually cut out the fur fabric pieces with the pile running in the wrong direction, the look of your toy could be ruined.

If you wish to make your design larger than the suggested size, simply draw the squares bigger; if you double the size of the squares you will double the size of the pattern. Similarly, you can reduce the final pattern size by drawing your grid smaller than suggested.

Using Your Pattern

For some projects, we suggest you use the squared up paper pattern for creating the design. You can either cut the pattern into individual pieces, as for the appliqué work, or trace it off on to your craft material using carbon paper. For other projects, such as the soft toy designs, we suggest you make cardboard templates of the pattern. This is because the fur fabrics used in toymaking are too thick to pin paper pattern pieces on to. Instead, you can use the cardboard templates to trace the shapes directly on to the reverse of your fabric using a felt-tip pen. Templates are much easier to trace around than paper patterns and they will last longer if you wish to use them several times.

Materials and Equipment

To help you prepare for your craft work, we have provided lists of the materials and equipment that will be required to make each design. Always try to buy good quality materials, particularly fabric and wools because, although they may be more expensive than inferior products, the end results will be so much better. Similarly, always buy good quality paint brushes; if you care for them properly they should outlive any cheaper varieties.

TEDDY GIFT WRAP AND GREETING CARDS

Make your own selection of wrapping paper, tags and cards to give a personal touch to your presents. There are cards to suit all kinds of occasions, from Christmas and birthdays to children's tea parties, and the wrapping paper is easily decorated using simple potato-printing.

Finish off your hand-made cards and tags with purchased bows, stars and ribbon. You can also use the pattern shapes to create your own designs.

Gift Box Greeting Card

To make this pretty card, first square up the gift box pattern shown opposite using a 2.5cm (1in) grid, referring to instructions on page 7. Cut the shape out of thin white cardboard. Trace off the other pieces, including the bear and the bow. If you wish to make several cards, make cardboard templates of the shapes so you can use them repeatedly. Now follow steps one and two.

Christmas Stocking Card

Enlarge the stocking pattern on page 9, reversing the image along the dotted line. Transfer the shape on to the reverse of some shiny red cardboard and cut it out. Put a little glue along the curved edge, then fold the stocking in half. Enlarge the pattern for the stocking top and cut it out of white cardboard. Fold it in half widthways and stick it across the top of the stocking, leaving the top open.

To make the base card, cut out a rectangle of green cardboard 17.5×7.5cm (7×3in) and fold it in half. Cut out some holly leaves and berries from cardboard and stick them to the stocking toe. Now glue the stocking to the base card. Make two yellow bears and decorate them with a bow, eyes and other features. Pop one bear into the top of the stocking along with some cardboard 'parcels' and glue the other to the heel.

8

1 *Using spray adhesive, cover both sides of the box shape with a piece of gift wrap and fold the box in half. Cut a rectangle 17.5×7.5cm (7×3in) from plain cardboard and fold it in half to form the base card. Use your other templates to cut the bear, bow, ribbon and miniature card shapes out of coloured cardboard, not forgetting the bear's bow tie.*

2 *Stick the side and base of the folded gift box together, leaving the top open. Score lines on the bow to represent the folds, using a sharp pencil. Glue the ribbon and bow across one corner of the box and stick the box to the base card. Stick the tiny card to the bear's paw and the bow tie in place and draw in the features with a silver ink pen.*

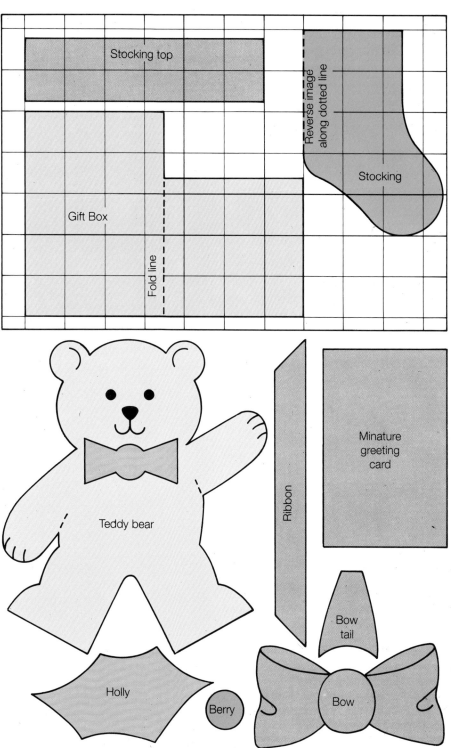

Stocking top

Reverse image along dotted line

Stocking

Gift Box

Fold line

Teddy bear

Ribbon

Minature greeting card

Holly

Berry

Bow tail

Bow

Above: *Folded concertina-style, this row of bears makes a simple but effective card.*

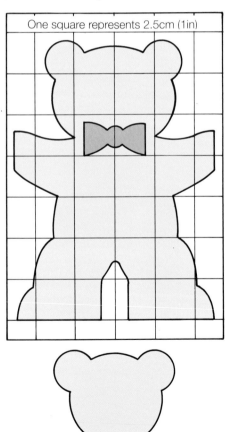

One square represents 2.5cm (1in)

Concertina Card

Enlarge the pattern on the left using a 2.5cm (1in) grid, then transfer the design to the reverse side of a long piece of coloured cardboard. Draw a row of four bears, joining their paws at either side. Cut out the row of teddy bears with a craft knife and fold them concertina-style where the paws join. Decorate each bear with a small bow, cut from shiny cardboard, and add features if you wish, using a metallic ink pen.

Jolly Bear Gift Wrap and Tag

Make a tracing of the bear's head shown below left. Transfer the design on to some thin cardboard and cut out the shape with a craft knife. Cut a medium-sized potato in half with a sharp knife, then follow steps one and two to print the paper. When the paint has dried, draw a small bow under each head using a metallic ink pen. Using the same pen, make dots all over the paper between the rows of heads.

To make the tag, fold a small rectangle of gold cardboard in half. Open it out again and transfer the bear head shape on to the reverse of one side. Cut around the shape with a craft knife. On the right side, draw a small bow under the bear's head. Finally, make a small hole in one corner and thread with gold cord.

1 *Trace the head outline on to the cut surface of the potato with a felt-tip pen. Cut along this line, holding the knife vertically. Then, with the knife held horizontally, trim away the excess potato around the design, leaving the head shape in the centre. Using a cocktail stick, make small holes to suggest the ears, eyes, mouth and nose.*

2 *Mix up the required shade of acrylic or poster paint in a shallow dish. Using a small brush, paint the colour generously over the raised design area. Turn the potato over and press it firmly on to some scrap paper, experimenting a few times before starting to print the gift wrap. When you are ready, print the design in rows on a large sheet of white paper.*

BABY BEAR MOBILE

This charming mobile, delightfully decorated with a wealth of pink bows, is guaranteed to delight any baby or small child. We have used pretty pastel shades but, for a different effect, bold primary colours could be used instead. As with any mobile, be sure to place it well out of the reach of tiny, grasping hands.

You will need:
Felt, one square each of the following
  colours: blue, yellow, pink, and
  peach
Matching sewing threads
Thin cardboard
Polyester filling
Glue
4 circular bag handles with 12.5cm
  (5in) diameter, and 1 with 17cm
  (6½in) diameter
Ribbon in the following lengths:
  6m (6yd) of 2.5cm (1in) wide white;
  1m (1yd) of 5mm (¼in) wide white;
  1m (1yd) of 5mm (¼in) wide blue;
  1m (1yd) of 2.5cm (1in) wide pink;
  1m (3yd) of 5mm (¼in) wide pink;
2 lengths of white cord, 60cm (24in)
  long

Felt is the ideal fabric for this project as it does not fray and is easy to cut. Squares of felt are readily available in a whole range of attractive colours from most department stores and craft shops.

Plastic bag handles form the basis for the mobile. Choose handles which are completely smooth around the edges as this will make them easier to bind with ribbon. Alternatively, if such handles are not available to you, lengths of cane can be used. Twist the cane round to form a hoop and tape the ends firmly together; wide brown parcel tape is ideal for this purpose.

The delightful bears can also be used to make a pram or cot toy. Either sew a piece of ribbon to the top of a single bear by which to hang it or string several bears together with elastic to stretch across the cot. If the bears are within baby's reach, however, you must ensure that any ribbon is firmly stitched in place to prevent an accident.

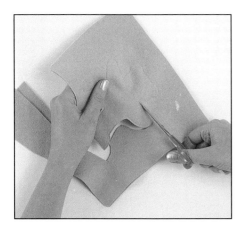

1 *Trace off the bear pattern on page 13 and transfer the design on to a piece of thin cardboard. Place the cardboard on to a double layer of felt and draw round the shape faintly with a sharp pencil. Pin the two layers together and machine sew all round. Cut around the shape close to the stitching, taking care not to cut the stitches.*

2 *Make four little bears in this way, each in a different pastel shade. On one side of each bear, carefully snip a slit across the neck with a pair of sharp scissors. Stuff the bears lightly, pushing the filling gently into the arms and legs with the end of a pencil. Using a matching thread, neatly oversew the gap.*

3 *Following the bear pattern for position, embroider the face on to each bear with stranded dark brown embroidery thread. Use French knots for the eyes, satin stitch for the nose, and back stitch for the mouth (see pages 24 and 31.) Tie a piece of narrow ribbon around the neck and finish with a bow.*

4 *Now cover each bag handle with the wide white ribbon. To start, tape one end of the ribbon to the ring to hold it in place. Now wind the ribbon tightly round the ring, overlapping at each turn. When you finally reach the beginning again, continue to wind a couple of times. Cut the ribbon, fold the raw end under and overstitch the ribbon in place.*

Below: *Trace off the full-size shape of the bear and make a cardboard template. Use this to cut out the bears from felt. You could also use the shape to make a matching stencil to decorate the cot.*

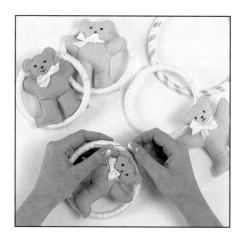

5 *Once the large ring has been completely bound, bind it with narrow blue ribbon to create a candy stripe effect. To start, turn under the raw edge of the blue ribbon and oversew it to the white ribbon. Then wind the ribbon around the ring, leaving a small space between each turn. Now sew each bear by its hands and feet to a small ring, using ladder stitch.*

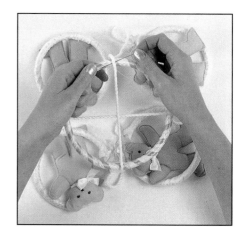

6 *Knot the ends of the cord and sew each end to a small ring. Sew small pink bows above the knots. Cross one cord over the top of the large ring, positioning it so that one bear hangs lower than the other. Sew the cord to the ring at each side. Repeat with the other cord and attach wide pink bows at the joins. Finally, suspend the mobile by a length of ribbon.*

BUTTONS AND BEARS

A self-coloured modelling material called Fimo has been used to make these delightful bears. Readily available from craft shops, it's both clean and easy to mould, and to harden it you simply bake it in the oven. Here we have made brooches, buttons and fridge magnets, but the same techniques can be used to make any number of fun designs.

The large bear heads, complete with hats, bows and scarves, make lovely brooches and go well with the baby bear buttons. The bears munching away on fruit and cake make amusing fridge magnets.

1 *To make the brooch, take a piece of beige Fimo and knead it until it is soft and pliable. Shape the muzzle and form two ears by pulling the Fimo gently between your thumb and finger. With the end of a blunt tool, poke a small indent in each ear to define the ear shape. Prepare a small ball of beige Fimo and press this on to the head to form the neck.*

Follow steps one to four to make the bear brooch with the hat and scarf. To make the bear with the green bow, follow steps one and two. Then roll out a long piece of green Fimo and flatten it with a rolling pin. Neaten the edges with a sharp knife to make an even strip of 'ribbon'. Cut off a small piece to wrap around the bear's neck and another two pieces to form the tails of the bow. Now make a ring with a longer section and press it together in the centre to form the two loops of the bow. Wrap a small piece of Fimo around the centre of the loops and press the bow under the bear's chin, on top of the 'tails'.

For the other designs, refer to the photograph opposite. (The buttons are made by piercing holes through the nose of a flat bear head shape.)

Finishing Off

Once you have finished modelling the bears, lay them on a clean baking sheet and bake them for about 20 minutes in a

You will need:
Fimo modelling material in the following colours: ochre, red, white, blue and green
Blunt modelling tool
Sharp needle
Sharp knife
Rolling pin
Fimo varnish
Fine paint brush
Brooch pins
Small magnets

pre-heated oven at 130°C/250°F/Gas Mk ½. Remove the bears from the oven and allow them to cool on a flat surface. Then, using a fine paint brush, dab a little Fimo varnish on to the eyes, nose, hats and bows to make them shine; leave the 'fur' in its natural matt finish. Finally, glue brooch pins or small magnets to the backs of the bears.

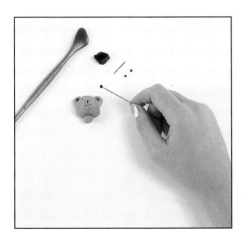

2 *With a large needle, make holes for the eyes and nose; mark a line where the mouth will be. Knead a small piece of black Fimo until soft and make three tiny balls for the eyes and nose. Press these gently into position. Roll a long thin black piece and place it into position for the mouth. With a sharp needle, mark tiny lines across the head to suggest the fur.*

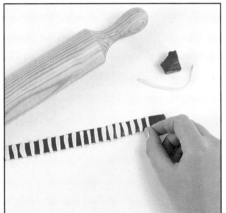

3 *To make the striped scarf, roll a long sausage piece of red Fimo and flatten it. Roll a thinner piece of white Fimo and cut it into small sections, the width of the red scarf. Place the sections on to the red strip, at regular intervals, and roll with a rolling pin to flatten. Using a sharp knife, neaten the edges of the scarf. Now make a striped hat to match.*

4 *Score lines down the scarf and hat with a needle to suggest ribbing. Cut off a short length of scarf. Wrap the long strip round the neck, overlapping one end over the other and bringing it downwards. Place the short length of scarf under the chin on top of the first section. Place the hat on the bear and add small white balls to the hat and ends of the scarf.*

REFLECTIONS

In this fun design, a plain mirror has been transformed by a cheerful teddy holding a set of brightly coloured balloons. The stained glass effect has been achieved using glass paints – which have a lovely translucent finish – and a special outliner paste which prevents the different colours from running into each other.

You will need:
Framed mirror
Felt-tip pen suitable for drawing on glass
Glass paints in the following colours: red, yellow, blue and green
Black outliner paste
Paint brush
Brush cleaner

Transparent glass paints are available from art and craft shops in a wide range of colours. They are simple to use and, as you can see, very effective. Always read the manufacturer's instructions before commencing with the work.

It is best to work in a dust-free area, and you should ensure that the mirror is cleaned before starting. First, enlarge the pattern on page 18 as necessary – according to the size of your own mirror

– and prepare thin cardboard templates of the balloons and bear. Now procede with steps one and two.

Before tackling step three, practise on a spare piece of glass – you will find a steady hand is needed to use the outliner paste, which is supplied in a tube. Squeeze the tube with equal pressure throughout the procedure and apply the paste in a continuous thin line, without any breaks. Leave the work to dry thoroughly before painting the mirror as described in step four.

Lay the mirror flat when applying the colours and clean the brush thoroughly before using another shade. While the paints are drying, keep the mirror away from dust or fluff which would mar the finished result.

1 *Clean the mirror carefully, then position the templates of the balloons and the bear on to the mirror, referring to the photograph. With a very fine felt-tip pen, draw an outline around the templates. We have placed the balloons directly above the bear's head but they could be at the top for a different effect.*

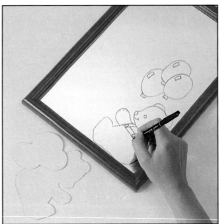

2 *Remove the templates and carefully draw in the details of the balloons and the bear's clothes, following the pattern. Leave the balloon strings until later as it is best to draw these in freehand using the outliner paste. Finally, draw in the flowers at the bottom left hand corner and the grassline across the base.*

3 *Starting with the balloon on the right, follow the shape with the outliner paste. Keep a firm pressure on the tube and continue all around the balloon. Repeat with the other balloons, and fill in the details. Working from the top, continue to outline the bear, grassline and flowers. Finish with the balloon strings.*

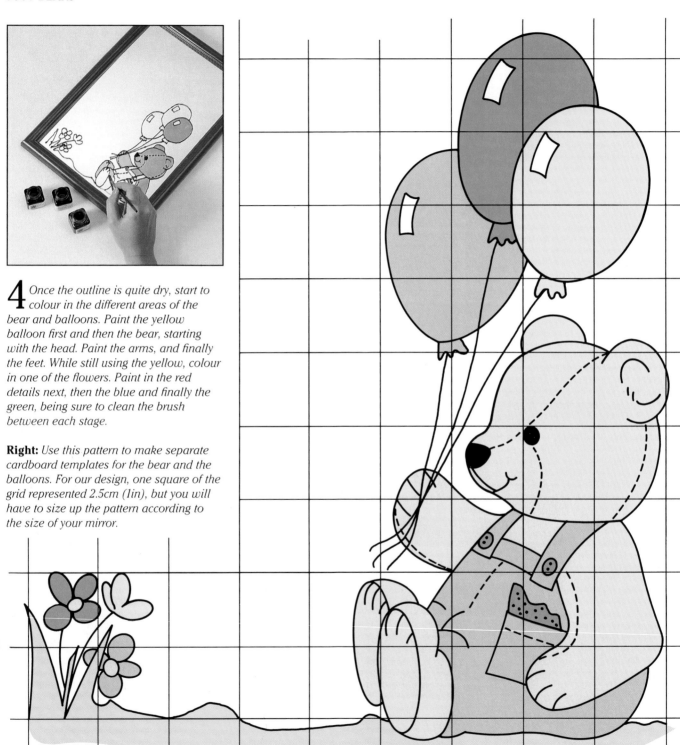

4 Once the outline is quite dry, start to colour in the different areas of the bear and balloons. Paint the yellow balloon first and then the bear, starting with the head. Paint the arms, and finally the feet. While still using the yellow, colour in one of the flowers. Paint in the red details next, then the blue and finally the green, being sure to clean the brush between each stage.

Right: Use this pattern to make separate cardboard templates for the bear and the balloons. For our design, one square of the grid represented 2.5cm (1in), but you will have to size up the pattern according to the size of your mirror.

LITERARY BEARS

Making wooden toys can be great fun and these charming bookends provide an ideal starting point for beginners. But, if you are in any doubt about using a fretsaw, we recommend you enlist the help of a friend with the right experience, leaving you free to enjoy painting the bears and assembling the bookends.

We have used pieces of pine for this project, which is easily available in the correct width from DIY shops. Following steps one and two, cut the various lengths of wood with a tenon saw. Choose a good wood glue to join the bases together. To hold the pieces in place while the glue is drying, try using a couple of strong, wide elastic bands.

Cut the bear shapes with a handheld fretsaw. Small table fretsaws, no larger than a sewing machine, are readily available from hobby shops. Buying one could be worthwhile if you feel that it could be used regularly enough to justify the cost. Otherwise, you could hire one from a tool hire shop.

Working with a handheld fretsaw needs a little practise for good results so, if you are not used to using one, experiment first on some spare wood.

Making Up the Bookends

Once you are ready to paint the bears, follow steps three and four. If you choose a non-toxic enamel hobby paint for this project it will not be necessary to prime the wood first. Available in small tins in a whole range of colours, hobby paints are durable and have a good finish. Be sure to clean your brushes carefully between each colour, and after the project is completed, using white spirit. As an alternative to tins, small spray cans of hobby paint are available in a limited range of colours, and these are useful when painting the bases.

When step four has been completed, glue the bears on to the bookends and leave to dry thoroughly. Follow step five to make the tiny books and mug, and glue these pieces to the bookends at the side of the bears. As long as the bookends are not for a small child, other items can also be added, using small scraps of wood and your imagination. Finally, stick non-slip sticky pads to the bases of the bookends.

You will need:

Pine wood: 2 pieces 14×9×2cm (5¾×3¾×¾in); 2 pieces 10×9×2cm (4×3¾×¾in); 2 pieces 12×10×2cm (5×4×¾in); 2 pieces 3×4.5×1cm (1¼×1¾×½in)
Thick dowelling, 5cm (2in) long
Tenon saw and fretsaw
Sandpaper
Wood glue
Non-toxic enamel paints in green, red, white, blue, yellow, black and beige
White spirit
Fine brush for detail, larger brush for areas
Small piece of wire
8 non-slip pads for bases

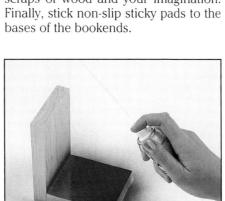

1 *From a 2cm (¾in) thick piece of pine, cut two pieces 14×9cm (5¾×3¾in) and two 10×9cm (4×3¾in), using a tenon saw. Sand the wood until smooth, then glue one long and one short piece together with wood glue to form an L-shape. Repeat with the other two pieces. Paint the bookends green and leave to dry.*

2 *Trace off the bear patterns on page 21 and transfer each one on to a piece of wood 12×10×2cm (5×4×¾in) using carbon paper. Line the back of the head and the base of the bear up against the straight edges of the wood. Now cut out the shape with a fretsaw. Using fine grade sandpaper, sand the shapes until smooth.*

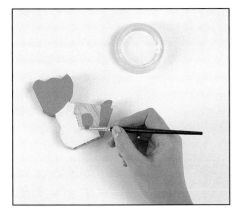

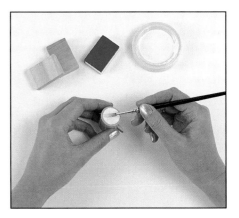

3 *Paint the areas for the head, hands and feet, including the edges of the wood. Also paint the back of the bear beige, unless you wish to colour in the details on the reverse. Let the paint dry, then apply a second coat if necessary. Change the colour to white and paint in the area of the pyjamas.*

4 *Now paint the book red, including the front edge. Leave to dry thoroughly. Next, using a fine paint brush and black paint, carefully add all the details to the bear, referring to the pattern. Once this has dried, change colour to medium blue and paint the stripes on the pyjamas.*

5 *Make tiny books using the small wooden blocks. Paint the pages white before painting the cover. Cut a small length of dowelling to make a mug, forming a handle from a piece of thick wire. Glue the ends of the wire into small holes in the side of the mug. Paint the sides of the mug yellow and the top white.*

Here is your full size pattern for the bear bookends. If you want to make the bears larger, don't forget to increase the size of the L-shaped bases as well.

BEARS ON THE WING

Blaze a trail across the bedroom wall with these fearless flying bears, made from felt in a range of bright colours. Neatly finished on the back, the bears could also be suspended from the ceiling in the form of a colourful mobile.

You can either arrange these delightful flying bears in a tight flight formation, as here, or in a line with the planes arranged in decreasing size.

You will need:
Red felt: 4 pieces 25×40cm (10×16in)
30cm (12in) squares of felt in each of
    the following colours: 4 green; 4
    orange; 1 blue; 1 white and 2 beige
30cm (⅜yd) of lightweight terylene
    wadding
One packet of tear-off backing for
    embroidery (e.g. 'Stitch 'n' Tear')
One packet of bonding web
Sticky pads for fixing to wall
Perlé embroidery thread in white
Matching sewing threads (except
    beige), plus black

Thick, good quality felt has been used for this project, and terylene wadding gives the planes a nice padded appearance. The use of tear-off backing fabric makes the edges slightly firmer which helps to keep the planes in shape.

To start, prepare templates for the three different sizes of plane using thin cardboard. Then follow steps one to four. For the machine satin stitch, set your machine to a close, medium zigzag setting and experiment first on scrap material until you are satisfied with the result. At the end of each section, pull through the top thread to the back and tie off firmly.

Once step four has been completed, tear the backing paper away from the plane. Similarly, once the propellor has been made in step five, tear away the backing paper before sewing the propellor to the end of the plane with a few ladder stitches. Cut small circles of contrasting felt for the wing rondels and stick them on to bonding web. Cut out the shapes, tear off the paper backing and iron the rondels to the wings.

When you have made up the bear as described in step six, make him a scarf by cutting a piece of felt 15×2.5cm (6×1in) and snipping a fringe at either end. Cut a small slit between the bear's neck and raised arm and slip the scarf through. Tie the scarf to one side.

1 *With a sharp pencil, draw around the plane template on to two layers of red felt, then mark the cockpit area. Bond the wing and tail plane pieces to a piece of bonding web and cut them out. Peel off the paper backing and place the pieces into the correct position on the plane. Iron in place to bond the felt together.*

2 *Pin the two layers of red felt together. Then, using a machine satin stitch and matching thread, sew around the line of the cockpit and across the top of the lower wing. With a pair of sharp-pointed scissors, carefully cut away the felt from inside the cockpit, keeping close to the stitching but without cutting the threads.*

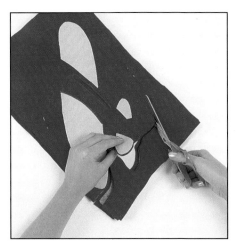

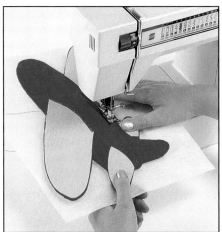

3 *Place the two layers of felt on to a third layer, a piece of terylene wadding and then a final layer of felt, making five layers in total. Pin or tack in place. Using a straight stitch and matching thread, machine sew around the plane, following the pencilled outline. Cut around the plane, close to the stitching.*

4 *Place the plane on to a piece of tear-off backing that is cut slightly larger than the plane itself. Starting at the point where the leading edge of the lower wing touches the main body, satin stitch around the red parts of the plane. Change the colour of thread to match the wings and sew around the remaining areas.*

EMBROIDERY STITCHES

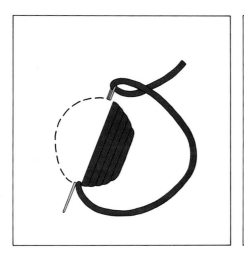

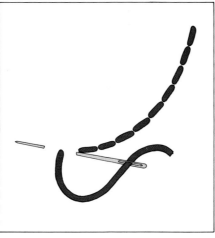

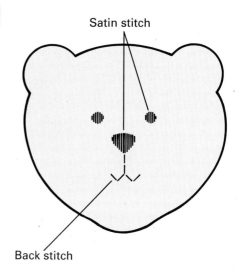

Satin Stitch

Satin stitch needs to be worked evenly to avoid puckering the fabric. Work straight stitches side by side to fill the shape, arranging them close together so they completely cover the fabric.

Back Stitch

Work back stitch with a forward and backward motion, as shown, keeping the stitches small and even. The finished result should give a fine, neat line rather like machine stitching.

Above: *Follow this diagram to embroider the faces on your bears.* **Right:** *To make all three planes, size up the pattern three times – once using a grid of 2.5cm (1in) squares, once with 2cm (¾in) squares and once with 1.7cm (⅝in) squares.*

5 *Draw the propellor on to a double layer of green felt. Pin the felt together with wadding in between. Using straight stitch, sew around the outline. Cut out the propellor, place it on to a piece of tear-off backing and satin stitch around the edge.*

6 *Draw the bear on to a double layer of beige felt. Place wadding between the layers and machine sew using straight stitch and black thread, following the pencil lines. Cut out the bear and sew the features referring to the illustration.*

Making the Clouds

Make a template of the cloud out of cardboard (using the largest grid size). Then, on a double layer of white felt, lightly trace out the shape of the cloud three times. Place a piece of terylene wadding between the layers, and pin them together. Machine sew with a straight stitch round the outlines, and cut out the shapes close to the stitching. Place the clouds on to a piece of tear-off backing fabric and neatly satin stitch round the edges using white thread.

Using a large embroidery needle, thread the clouds on to a length of white perlé embroidery thread. Sew one end of the thread to the last cloud, and the other to the back of the smallest plane. Evenly space the other two clouds.

To finish, attach sticky pads to the back of each plane and each cloud. peel off the backing and place the planes in position on the wall.

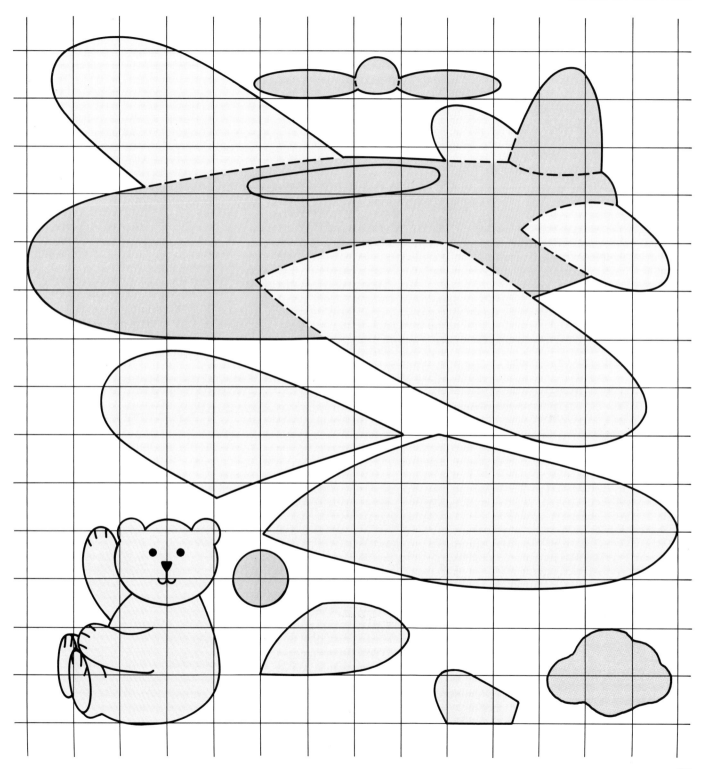

PARTY TIME

Next time you hold a tea party for the kids, why not give it a bear theme with this wonderful novelty cake and some tasty gingerbread cookies? The sugar paste bears are easier to make than you might think. Use your favourite recipe for the cake and either make your own sugar paste or buy it ready made to save time.

Modelling with sugar paste is not too difficult and can be very effective. A large range of concentrated paste colours are available from specialist shops and mail order suppliers; ordinary food colours are not suitable. The colour should be added a bit at a time and the paste kneaded thoroughly. Colour all the paste that is needed in one batch as it is difficult to match up the colour again.

Once you have made the cake, following steps one to six, why not make some place markers using the same little sugar paste bears? Cut a circle of white paste and let it dry. Then make a bear from the paste and assemble it in a sitting position in the centre of the circle. Place a small 'gift' next to the bear and a cocktail stick in the paw with the child's name attached on a piece of paper.

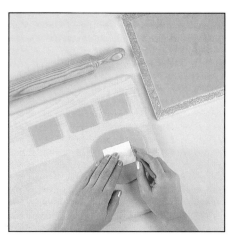

1 *Make up 1.125kg (2½lb) of sugar paste according to the recipe above. Colour 450g (1lb) of sugar paste pink and wrap the rest in cling film (plastic wrap) until later. Cover a cake board with a square of pink paste. Roll out more paste and, using a cardboard template, cut four small rectangles for place mats. Wrap up the remaining paste with cling film.*

2 *Prepare a 20cm (8in) round cake and cover with marzipan if desired. Centre the cake on the board and, if the cake has been marzipanned, brush with a little water. If not using marzipan, brush the cake with warmed and sieved apricot jam. Roll out 450g (1lb) of white sugar paste into a circular piece large enough to cover the top and sides of the cake.*

3 *With the help of a rolling pin, drape the paste over the cake and allow it to hang in folds down the sides like a tablecloth. Gently push the folds into place and cut away any excess with a sharp knife. Roll out some more paste and cut five small hexagonal shapes for plates, using a cutter. Stick four plates on to the placemats, using a little water to stick.*

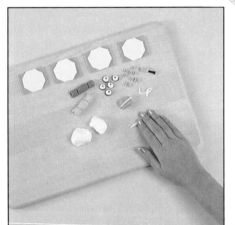

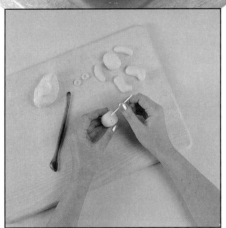

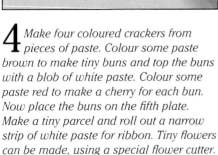

4 *Make four coloured crackers from pieces of paste. Colour some paste brown to make tiny buns and top the buns with a blob of white paste. Colour some paste red to make a cherry for each bun. Now place the buns on the fifth plate. Make a tiny parcel and roll out a narrow strip of white paste for ribbon. Tiny flowers can be made, using a special flower cutter.*

5 *Make four little bears, each in a different colour. The bears are basically the same shape but have been positioned differently on the cake. Colour the paste as desired. Then model an oval piece for the body, two curved arms, two legs and a pair of ears. Roll a ball of paste for the head and shape the muzzle. Poke eyes and nose with a cocktail stick.*

6 *Assemble the bears using a little water to stick. (This can be left to the end if you prefer, with the bears constructed in position on the cake itself.) Now make four stools out of coloured paste. The base of the stool is a tubular piece of paste and the top can be cut using a cutter. Finally, once all the elements are dry, position them as desired on the cake.*

GINGERBREAD BEAR RECIPE

225g (8oz, 2 cups) plain flour
1 level tsp baking powder
2 level tsps ground ginger
½ level tsp bicarbonate of soda
85g (3oz, ⅓ cup) margarine or
  butter
85g (3oz, ⅓ cup) moist brown
  sugar
85g (3oz, ⅓ cup) golden syrup
170g (6oz, 1½ cups) icing sugar, to
  decorate

Sift the dry ingredients together.
Cream the margarine or butter,
sugar and syrup until soft and light
in texture. Work in the dry
ingredients and knead the mixture
thoroughly.

Dust your work surface with
flour and roll out the dough to a
thickness of 5mm (¼in). Now
follow step seven (right).

Transfer the biscuits to lightly
greased baking trays. Bake in the
centre of a hot oven, 210°C/425°F/
Gas Mk 6-7, for 10 minutes. Leave
to cool on the baking trays. When
the biscuits are cool, pipe the
eyes, nose and mouth using the
icing sugar blended with a little
warm water to give a flowing
consistency. Leave the icing to set.

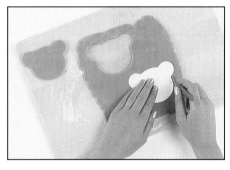

7 *To make a template for the cookies, refer to the photograph below, scaling it up as necessary. Trace the shape on to thin cardboard and cut it out. Roll out the dough, dust the surface with flour and place the template on top. Cut around the shape with a sharp knife.*

To continue the bear theme, you can
also make some teddy bear cookies out
of gingerbread. Follow the recipe on the
left and refer to step seven to cut out the
head shapes.

Making the Table Mats
To complete each party place setting,
make a set of mats in co-ordinated
colours. Enlarge the pattern on this page
to the correct size using a 2.5cm (1in)
grid and referring to page 7. Choose
shiny cardboard for the mat and transfer
the bear pattern on to the reverse side
using carbon paper. Cut out the shape
with a craft knife. 'Self-healing' cutting
mats are available to protect your working surface and are recommended when
using a craft knife.

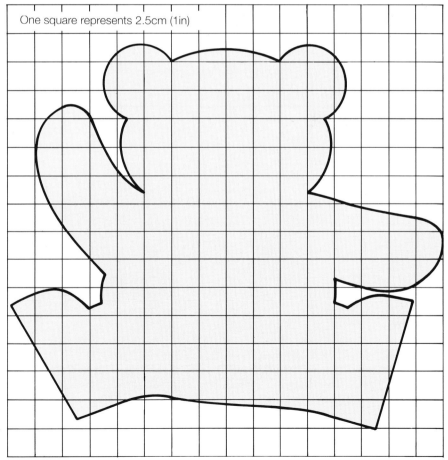

One square represents 2.5cm (1in)

NURSERY SAMPLER

This simple design worked in cross and three-quarter cross stitch, and edged in Holbein stitch, is easy enough for anyone to tackle. It makes an ideal accessory for a traditional-style nursery but would equally delight any adult lover of bears.

You will need:
40×45cm (16×18in) rectangle of white even-weave linen
1 skein of stranded cotton thread in each of the following colours: blue, yellow, purple, red, green, black, dark brown and light brown
Crewel needle
Embroidery hoop or frame

EMBROIDERY STITCHES

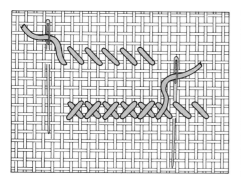

Cross Stitch
First, work a row of diagonal stitches from right to left of the shape being covered. Then work the top diagonals, moving back in the opposite direction.

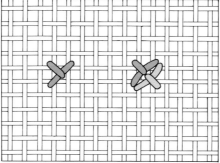

Three-quarter Cross Stitch
This stitch is worked in the same way as full cross stitch except the second stitch is only half the length of the first. It can be worked back to back in two colours.

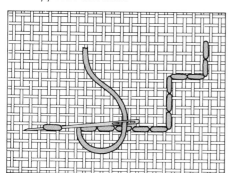

Holbein Stitch
Work a row of evenly spaced stitches along the edge of the shape, stepping the row as necessary. Fill in the spaces by working back in the opposite direction.

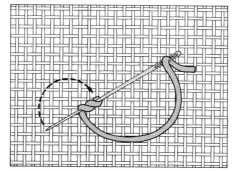

French Knot
Holding the thread taut on the surface, twist the needle around it two or three times. Tighten the twists, turn the needle and insert it back into the fabric.

This sampler has been worked on even-weave linen, a fabric with excellent qualities of handling and durability. The use of the three-quarter cross stitch gives the illusion in places of rounded edges, an effect which is highlighted with the Holbein stitch outlines.

Begin by neatening the edges of the piece of linen, either by machining a zig-zag stitch around the edge or turning a single hem. It can be helpful in this type of embroidery to find the centre point. To do so, run a vertical and a horizontal line of tacking stitches halfway across the fabric; the centre is the point at which the lines cross.

Stretch the fabric in a large embroidery hoop or frame to keep the fabric grain straight. Using a hoop will ensure even and accurate stitching, and the work will only need a minimum amount of pressing on completion.

Working the Embroidery
Find the centre square on the chart on page 32 and start the embroidery on the corresponding point on your piece of fabric. Work outwards from the centre, using three strands of embroidery thread throughout. Once the bear family is completed, use Holbein stitch and black or dark brown embroidery thread to outline the shapes. Finally, add French knots for the eyes, mouths and buttons.

BEARS IN THE PANTRY

Give your kitchen a homely touch with these honey bears carrying freshly-baked pies. Painted with bright ceramic paints, they'll bring a splash of colour to plain white china. As well as mugs and plates, the design can be adapted to suit different utensils such as storage jars. You can also appliqué some matching napkins to complete the set.

Largely decorative, this hand-painted china is not suitable for regular use. Clean the china, then trace off the pattern on page 34, and transfer the design on to some low tack peel (adhesive film), available from art shops.

Follow steps one and two to decorate the mugs. Decorate the plate in the same way, arranging the bears around the edge. Finish off with a few extra designs between the bears. When the paint is dry, add a coat of ceramic varnish.

1 Cut out the bear and put the adhesive film on to a mug. Trace around the shape with a chinagraph pencil, then remove the film and add the features.

2 Paint the yellow areas first and, when dry, paint red lines on the bib to look like gingham. Paint the pie golden brown and, finally, paint the black outlines.

Making the Napkins

Choose a set of plain napkins in a bright colour for this design. Strong linen fabric gives the best results. For the bear appliqué, small scraps of cotton will be ideal.

Iron a piece of bonding web on to the reverse of the fabrics chosen for the bear appliqué. Trace off the bear shape from this page and transfer the pattern on to the backing paper of the bonding web, remembering to reverse the design. Do the same for the bib and the pie.

Now follow steps one to three to complete the appliqué. Use a black thread in your sewing machine and, for a good result, ensure that both the top and bobbin (shuttle) thread are the same colour. A medium-width close zig-zag stitch should be selected on your sewing machine. We recommend that you experiment with scraps of fabric before starting the project.

When the machining has been finished, embroider an eye and nose on the bear using black embroidery thread and a satin stitch, as described on page 24.

Use this full size pattern to cut out the fabric pieces for the appliqué work, being sure to cut a separate piece for the pie.

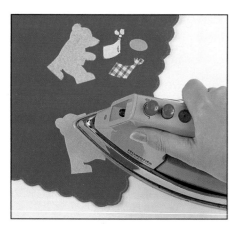

1 *Cut out the shapes of the bear, bib and pie, following the outline on the bonding web backing. Peel off the backing paper and place the bear into position on the corner of the napkin. Iron the motif on to the napkin, following the manufacturer's instructions. Place the pieces for the bib and pie to one side until later.*

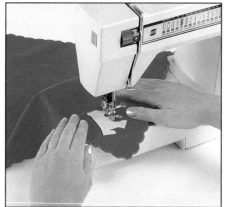

2 *Starting at the bear's foot, zig-zag stitch around the bear shape, carefully turning the work at sharp corners. When you reach the beginning again, pull through the loose ends of thread and secure them firmly on the reverse of the work. Machine sew around the arm. Now place the bib piece into position.*

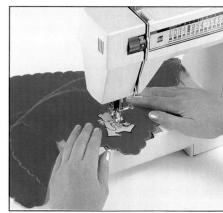

3 *Bond the bib to the appliqué and machine sew around the shape with the zig-zag stitch. Once this is done, stitch around the knot at the back of the bear's neck, referring to the pattern. Place the pie in position on top of the bear's hand and bond in place. Zig-zag stitch around the pie and across the bear's arm.*

CUSHIONED FOR COMFORT

This delightfully sleepy bear cushion has been made using appliqué – a simple sewing technique that gives a most attractive result. We've used a suede effect fabric for the bear itself which gives him a soft fur-like texture. If this is not available, try using needlepoint corduroy or velvet instead. Glazed cotton, with its rich sheen, makes a perfect choice for the cushion cover.

You will need:
60cm (⅝yd) green fabric
20cm (¼yd) beige fabric
20cm (¼yd) cream fabric
20cm (¼yd) peach fabric
3m (3yd) thick piping cord
20cm (¼yd) lightweight terylene
   wadding
50cm (18in) cushion pad
Sewing thread in peach, cream, green
   and brown
Zipper foot (to make piping)

Enlarge the pattern on page 39 to the correct size, using the method described in the introduction on page 7 and making each square on your grid 2.5×2.5cm (1×1in). Choose a pattern paper which is relatively lightweight yet strong enough to withstand the various pinholes.

Cut two squares of green fabric measuring 53cm (19¼in) square (including a 1.5cm, ⅝in seam allowance), and two strips of peach fabric measuring 150×5cm (54in×2in). (Adjust the length and number of strips according to the width of your fabric.) Now follows steps one and two. When machine sewing each part as described, always use a matching thread for a good finish.

Next, arrange the different pieces on one of the green squares. Start with the peach cushions, as described in step three. When following step four, as long as the inside edges of the cushions are covered by the bear's body you can experiment a little with the bear's position. For instance, tilt the head more to one side, and the bear looks more sleepy. Move the feet slightly for a different effect. Be sure you are satisfied with the position of each part before continuing with the next layer.

Using this method of appliqué, the bear will have a slightly padded appearance and there will be no raw edges, even though a straight stitch rather than satin stitch has been used around each

part. Always remember to pull the threads through to the back of the work and tie off securely to prevent the stitching coming undone.

Completing the Features
Once the bear has been sewn in place, attention can be paid to the bear's face. Position the nose on to the muzzle and sew it in place with the same satin stitch

as described in step five. Finally, embroider a few small French knots (see page 31) on to the bear's face using light brown embroidery thread.

1 *Pin the pattern pieces for the different parts of the design on to the appropriate fabrics. Carefully cut out each shape and pin each part, right side down, to the terylene wadding. Tack (baste) and carefully machine sew round each piece, using straight stitch, approximately 5mm (¼in) from the edge.*

2 *With a pair of small, sharp scissors, carefully cut a slit in the centre of the wadding 5cm (2in) long. Snip the curves where necessary and turn each part through to the right side, ensuring that all the curves and corners are pushed out. Press the pieces with a cool iron before assembling the design.*

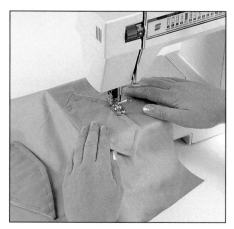

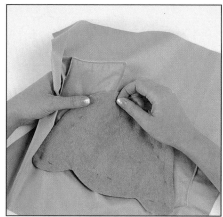

Making up the Cushion Cover

Join the two strips of peach fabric together to make one long piece. Fold the strip in half lengthways around the piping cord, with the fabric right side uppermost. Pin and machine sew close to the cord using a regular machine foot.

Pin one end of the fabric to the cord and then gather the fabric, adjusting the gathers evenly along the required length of 2.2m (6½ft). Now follow step six.

Place the two cushion pieces right sides together with the raw edges matching all round. Pin and tack around the edge, and then machine sew, using a zipper foot, close to the piping cord. Leave a gap of about 25cm (10in) to insert a cushion pad.

Snip the corners of the cushion cover before turning it the right way out. Press the cover, insert the cushion pad and carefully hand stitch the opening, using a ladder stitch. Alternatively, you could insert a zip so that the pad can be removed for cleaning.

3 *The appliqué is built up in layers, working from the base layer of the peach cushions to the paws. Lay all the pieces on the green cushion front and work out the position for the peach cushions. Pin the cushions into place, then tack (baste) them to the main green fabric. Using matching thread, sew all around, close to the edge.*

4 *Pin and tack (baste) the main bear body in position, referring to the photograph. The body should overlap the peach cushions. Sew into place as before, and continue to build up the body layers. The head should be sewn next, then the cream muzzle, tummy and feet. Always pin and tack (baste) each piece in place before stitching to ensure it lies flat.*

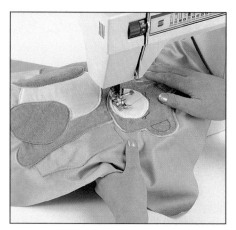

5 *Using a close medium-width satin stitch on the machine, now add the details to the bear. Choose a darker brown thread to contrast with the beige. Start at the head and work downwards from the face to the arm folds and tummy button. Finish at the feet by sewing four small lines on each foot and an inner circle of stitching to represent the pad.*

6 *Starting at the centre of one side, pin the covered piping cord around the edge of the cushion, matching up the raw edges. Where the ends meet, cut away the cord inside the fabric to avoid a lumpy join. Overlap the ends of the fabric slightly, turning them out towards the edge of the cushion. Machine sew all around, being sure to stitch over both ends of piping.*

Right: *Trace off the shapes for the bear and cushions on to squared paper, making each square represent 2.5cm (1in). The design could also be used to decorate a child's cot or duvet cover.*

Above: *If peach and green doesn't match the decor of your room, try making the cushion in a different colour scheme.*

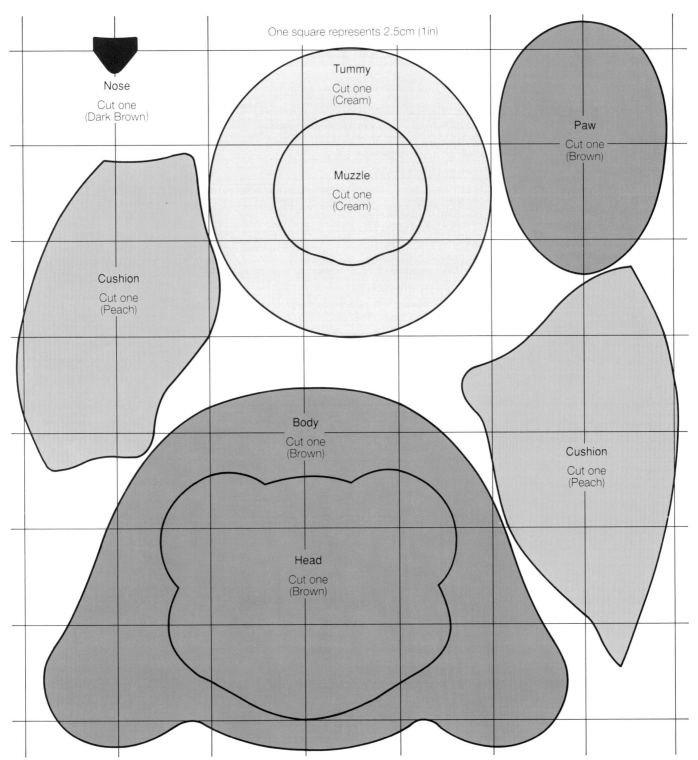

One square represents 2.5cm (1in)

Nose
Cut one
(Dark Brown)

Tummy
Cut one
(Cream)

Muzzle
Cut one
(Cream)

Paw
Cut one
(Brown)

Cushion
Cut one
(Peach)

Cushion
Cut one
(Peach)

Body
Cut one
(Brown)

Head
Cut one
(Brown)

WINTER WARMER

*K*nit this colourful and cosy teddy sweater to keep yourself warm this winter. The pattern comes in two sizes, to fit an 86-91cm (34-36in, size 1) chest or a 97-102cm (38-40in, size 2) chest and you can either knit it with the collar as here, or without as you prefer.

You will need:
9 (10)×50g (2oz) of DK pure new wool (we have used Patons) in main colour A (red)
3 balls of same in contrast colour B (white)
1 ball each of same in each of contrast colours C (grey), D (pink), E (green) and F (blue)
A pair each of 3¼mm (US size 3) and 4mm (US size 6) knitting needles

Measurements
To fit bust 86-91(97-102)cm/34-36 (38-40)in
Actual Measurements
Bust 102(114)cm/40(45)in
Length to shoulders 64(65)cm/25¼(25½in)
Sleeve seam 46cm/18in

Tension
22 sts and 28 rows to 10cm (4in) measured over spot patt worked on 4mm (6) needles

Below: *These are the measurements for the finished parts of the sweater.*

Abbreviations
K knit, **p** purl, **st(s)** stitch(es), **inc** increase(ing), **dec** decrease(ing), **M1** make 1 as follows: pick up loop between st just worked and next st on left-hand needle and k into back of it, **beg** begin(ning), **cont** continue, **patt** pattern, **rep** repeat.

Front
** Using 3¼mm (3) needles and A, cast on 99(109) sts.
Rib row 1 K1, * p1, k1, rep from * to end.
Rib row 2 P1, * k1, p1, rep from * to end.

Rep these 2 rows for 8cm (3¼in), ending with rib row 1.
Inc row Rib 4(2), * M1, rib 7, rep from * to last 4(2) sts, M1, rib to end. 113(125) sts. **
Change to 4mm (6) needles.
Join on and cut off colours as required. When working in spot patt, carry yarn not in use loosely across wrong side of work. For teddy motif, use separate

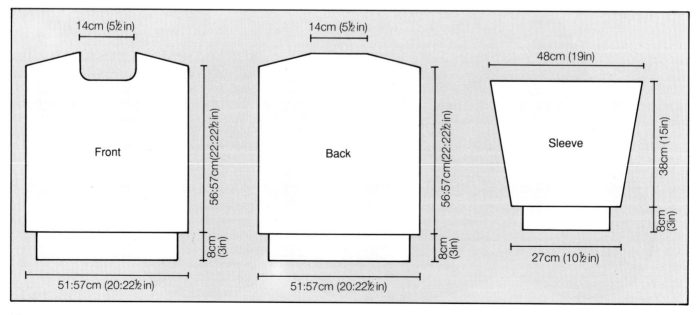

Above: *This photograph shows the detail of the design. Either follow our colour scheme or choose other colours to create a different effect.*

Far right: *Knit your teddy sweater in stocking stitch, following the design on the chart opposite square by square.*

balls of yarn for each area of colour and twist yarns together on wrong side of work when changing colour to avoid making a hole.
Reading odd numbered (k) rows from right to left and even numbered (p) rows from left to right, work in patt from chart as follows:
Row 1 With A, k to end.
Row 2 With A, p to end.
Row 3 K5A, * 1B, 5A, rep from * to end.

Row 4 P5A, * 1B, 5A, rep from * to end.
Beg with row 5, cont in patt from chart, shaping neck and shoulders as indicated and leaving 19 sts at front neck on a holder.

Back
Work as given for front from ** to **
Change to 4mm (6) needles.
Work in spot patt as follows:
Row 1 With A, k to end.
Row 2 With A, p to end.
Row 3 K2A, * 1B, 5A, rep from * to last 3 sts, k1B, 2A.
Row 4 With A, p to end.
Row 5 With A, k to end.
Row 6 With A, p to end.
Row 7 K5A, * 1B, 5A, rep from * to end.
Row 8 With A, p to end.
These 8 rows form the spot patt.
Cont in patt until back measures same

as front to shoulders, ending with a wrong-side row.
Shape shoulders
Cast off 10(12) sts at beg of next 6 rows, then 11 sts at beg of foll 2 rows. Cut off yarn leave rem 31 sts on a holder.

Sleeves
Using 3¼mm (3) needles and A, cast on 51 sts. Work 8cm (3¼in) rib as given for front, ending with rib row 1.
Inc row Rib 9, * M1, rib 5, rep from * to last 7 sts, M1, p7, 59 sts.
Change to 4mm (6) needles.
Working in spot patt as given for back, inc and work into patt 1 st each end of 9th and every foll 4th row until there are 105 sts. Work straight until sleeve measures 46cm (18in) from cast-on edge, ending with a wrong-side row. Cast off.

Neckband
Join right shoulder seam.
With right side facing, using 3¼mm (3) needles and A, pick up and k28 sts down left side of front neck, k19 sts from front neck holder, pick up and k28 sts up right side of front neck, then k31 sts from back neck holder. 106 sts. Work 5cm (2in) k1, p1 rib.
Cast off in rib.

Collar
Using 3¼mm (3) needles and A, cast on 121 sts.
Work 10cm (4in) rib as given for front welt.
Cast off in rib.

To make up
Join left shoulder and neckband seam. Fold neckband in half to wrong side and slip stitch into place. Placing side edges of collar to centre front, sew cast-on edge of collar to inside of neckband. Fold sleeves in half lengthwise, then placing folds at tops of sleeves to shoulder seams, sew into position. Join side and sleeve seams.

42

160
150
140
130
120
110
100
90
80
70
60
50
40
30
20
10

Size B
Size A

BEAR-FACED SWEATER SET

Suitable for children and adults alike, here's the perfect way to brighten up a plain sweater and scarf. This charming design has been made in appliqué, using a combination of fur fabric and satin for an interesting contrast of fabric textures.

You will need:
Matching sweater and scarf
Small piece of beige fur fabric
Small piece of green satin (or silk)
Sewing thread in black, gold and green
One packet of bonding web
Carbon paper

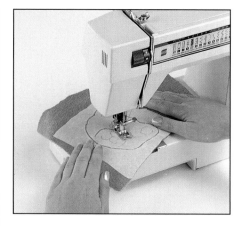

For this design you can either buy or knit a matching sweater and scarf, choosing a bright, bold colour.

To make the appliqué set, first copy the pattern of the bear's head and the bow on to a 2.5cm (1in) square grid, enlarging the pattern to the correct size using the method described on page 7. Bond a piece of bonding web to the reverse side of a piece of fur fabric that has been cut slightly larger than the head pattern. Using carbon paper, transfer the design to the backing paper.

Applying the Design
Once you have finished making both the head and bow pieces, according to the instructions in steps one to three, peel the backing paper from the reverse of the designs and place the head and bow on to the knitwear in the desired position. Cover the pieces with a damp cloth and press carefully with a hot iron to bond the fabrics together. Finally, using a small stitch, carefully oversew the appliqué shapes to the knitting around the edge of the work.

1 *Set your machine to a medium-width close zig-zag stitch. With the reverse side of the fur fabric uppermost, machine stitch around the outline of the head using gold thread. Sew around the curve of the muzzle and the inner ears. At the end of each row of stitching, pull the loose threads through to the back of the work and tie off.*

One square represents 2.5cm (1in)

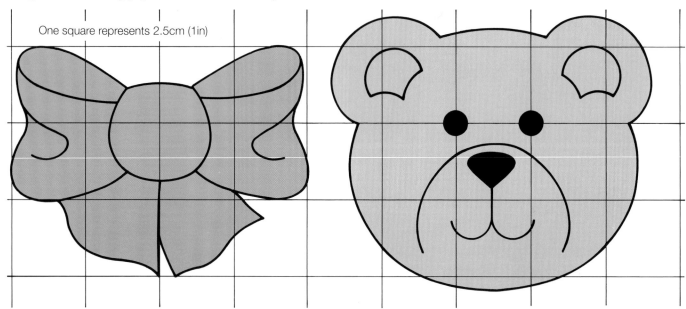

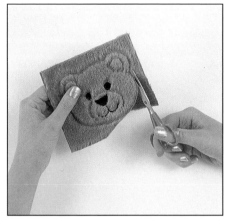

2 *Change the colour of thread in the machine to black. Then, still working on the reverse of the head, follow the lines for the mouth, starting at the nose. Next, use a larger zig-zag stitch to fill in the nose area and the eyes. Turn the work over to check that no parts have been missed. With small sharp scissors, cut around the edge of the head, close to the stitches.*

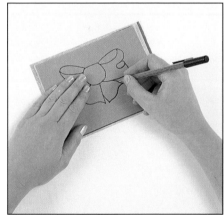

3 *Iron a piece of bonding web to a piece of green satin or silk, cut slightly larger than the bow pattern. Transfer the pattern to the reverse of the fabric using carbon paper, remembering to fill in all the details. With green thread and a medium-width zig-zag stitch, follow the outlines on the backing paper, filling in all the details. Cut around the shape as before.*

TEDDY BEARS' TEA PARTY

If you go down to the woods today you're sure of a big surprise . . . These traditional teddy bears, complete with simple clothes, are jointed so they can be made to sit up, wave and turn their heads. Scaled in three different sizes, you can make just one teddy bear or the complete set to enchant children of all ages.

You will need:

1m (1yd) beige fur fabric (for 3 bears)
Polyester filling
Safety eyes: 16.5mm for father bear, 13.5mm for the other two
Strong sewing thread
Joints: father bear – 2 pairs 55mm (for arms), 3 pairs 65mm; mother bear – 2 pairs 45mm (for arms), 3 pairs 55mm; baby bear – 2 pairs 35mm (for arms), 3 pairs 45mm
Teasel brush
Remnants of fabric, lace and tape for clothes
Ribbon
Black embroidery thread
Brown felt

Making a jointed bear is not as difficult as it first appears. We have used hardboard joint sets, but other types are also available from craft shops.

To make the mother bear, enlarge the pattern on page 50, making each square of your grid 2.5cm (1in). For father bear, make each square 2.8cm (1⅛in), and for baby bear, each square should be 2cm (⅞in). Prepare cardboard templates and mark out the shapes on to the reverse of your fur fabric, ensuring that the pile runs in the correct direction. For mother bear's apron, cut three pieces of checked fabric measuring 7cm (3in) square, 14×26cm (5½×10¼in) and 5×85cm (2×34in). Now follow steps one to eleven to make up the toy.

To make the mother bear, enlarge the pattern on page 50

USEFUL STITCHES

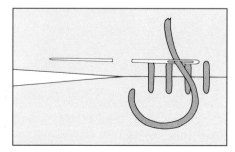

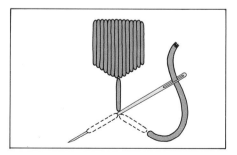

Ladder stitch (above) is used for closing · gaps in seams and for attaching the head to the body. Pull the stitches tight as you go so that they are barely visible.

To sew the nose and mouth, push the needle through from the base of the head to the top right corner of the nose. Now follow the diagram above to complete.

TOYMAKING TIPS

Always choose good quality fur fabrics.

Beginners should choose fur fabrics with a knitted backing; they stretch slightly and do not fray, making them easier to work with.

When positioning pattern templates on fabric, pay special attention to arrows indicating direction of pile.

Cut fur pieces out of single thickness fabric only.

Reverse the pattern template when cutting a second asymmetrical piece out of fur.

Always pin then tack (baste) a seam before you sew it by machine or hand.

Pin fur fabrics with glass headed pins as they are easier to find; pins left in toys cause a serious danger to children.

Sew fabric pieces together with right sides facing unless stated otherwise.

Use a strong sewing thread for sewing seams; one containing man-made fibres is best as it will stretch slightly.

Use a teasel brush to pull out fur trapped in seams.

Use a long blunt instrument such as a thick knitting needle or a Phillips screwdriver to help you turn your toy.

Sew heads on with ladder stitch, using strong button thread and a large darning needle; sew round at least twice to secure firmly.

Always use good quality filling – old stockings and scraps of fabric give a poor finished look to your toy.

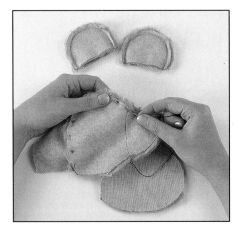

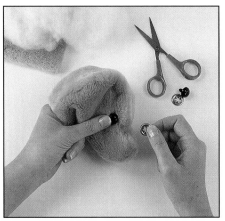

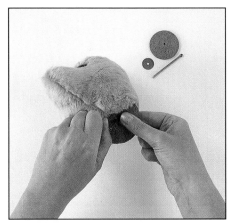

1 With right sides facing, sew the ears together in pairs, leaving the straight edge open. Place the two side head pieces right sides together and sew along seam A-B. Starting at point A, tack (baste) the head gusset into place on one side, easing the fabric as you go until D is reached. Tack the other side of the head to the gusset and sew around the whole shape.

2 Pierce tiny holes at the eye positions with the end of a pair of small sharp scissors and turn the head the right way out. Insert a pair of plastic safety eyes through the holes and secure on the reverse with the metal washer provided with the eyes. Inspect all the seams and stuff the head firmly, moulding it into a nicely rounded shape.

3 If you are using a hardboard joint set, with cotter pin and washers, first thread one washer on to the pin. Then place the hardboard disc on top. With the cotter pin facing outwards, push the disc into the base of the head, making sure it is centrally placed. Using strong thread and a running stitch, gather the neck edge of the bear and fasten off firmly.

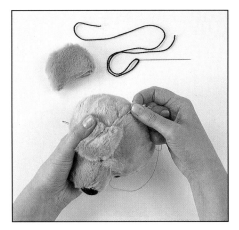

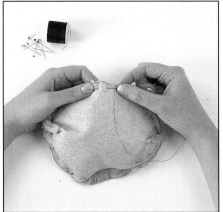

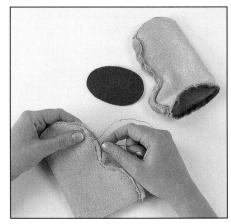

4 Referring to the illustration on page 47, embroider the nose and mouth using thick black embroidery thread. Turn the ears and oversew the raw edges. Hold one ear flat against the head as shown and oversew the ear in place with strong thread. Then lift the ear up and ladder stitch the back of the ear to the head. Repeat with the other ear.

5 Sew the darts on each side of the body and pierce the joint holes according to the pattern. Place the two body halves together, with right sides facing. Machine sew around the body shape, leaving a gap for turning at the back. Turn the body the right way out. It is easier to brush the seams with a teasel brush at this stage, before the arms and legs are attached.

6 Fold the legs in half. Sew around the curved edge, leaving a gap at the top of each leg and the straight bottom edge open. Sew the paw pads into place, easing the fabric as you work so that there are no tucks. Pierce a small hole in each leg at the position marked on the pattern. Turn the legs the right way out and check the seams carefully, especially the pad area.

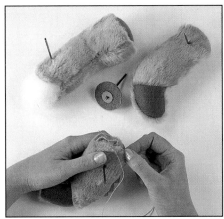

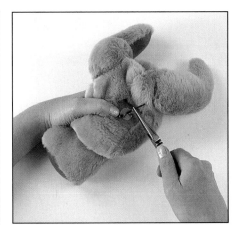

7 *Sew the paw pads to the end of the arms, between points E and F. Then fold the arms in half and, starting at point E, sew around each arm, easing the fabric as you work and leaving a gap at the top. Pierce the joint hole at the top of the arms at the point indicated. Turn the arms the right way out and inspect the seams. Stuff the arms and legs half way up the limbs.*

8 *Thread the washers and hardboard discs on to the cotter pins for the arms and legs. Poke the cotter pin through the hole made earlier, and lay the hardboard disc flat against the reverse of the fabric. The top of the disc should be below the level of the raw edge of the fabric. Add more stuffing until the limb is completely filled. Close the gap with a ladder stitch.*

9 *To assemble the bear, first take one limb and push the cotter pin through the appropriate hole in the body. Inside the body, thread another hardboard disc and then a washer on to the pin. Refer to the illustration below to secure the joint. Repeat the process with each limb and the head. Finally, stuff the body firmly and close the gap with a ladder stitch.*

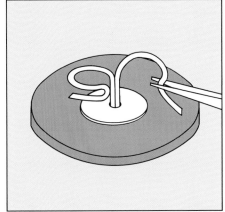

10 *To make the apron, first sew the pocket in place. Hem three sides and gather the top to 10cm (4in). With raw edges together, sew the strap to the top of the apron. Fold the strap in half, with right sides facing and close the raw edges between the apron and the strap ends. Turn the straps the right way out, fold the raw edges under and slip stitch closed.*

11 *For baby bear's bib, cut a circle of fabric measuring 8cm (3in) and cut across one side to form a straight edge. Sew some lace around the curved edge and a length of white cotton tape across the top, to tie around baby bear's neck. Finally, make a white handkerchief to pop in mother bear's apron and tie bright bows around the bears' necks.*

To secure the joint, first ease the prongs of the cotter pin apart using a pair of narrow pliers. Grasp one prong half way down with the pliers and bend it away from the centre until the tip reaches the hardboard disc. Now continue to bend the pin inwards, forming an R-shape as seen here. Repeat the procedure with the other side to hold the limb firmly in place.

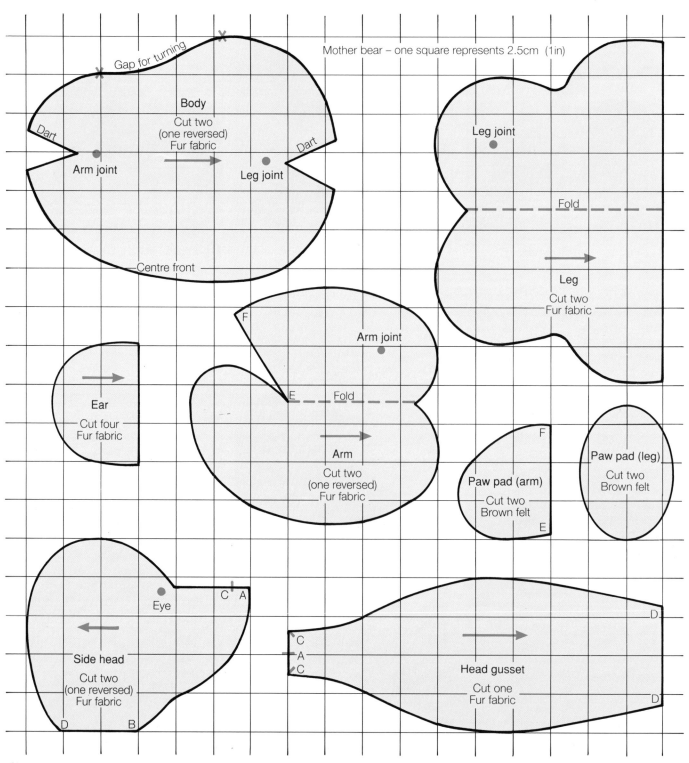

Mother bear – one square represents 2.5cm (1in)

Body
Cut two
(one reversed)
Fur fabric

Gap for turning

Dart

Arm joint

Leg joint

Dart

Centre front

Leg joint

Fold

Leg
Cut two
Fur fabric

F

Arm joint

E Fold

Ear
Cut four
Fur fabric

Arm
Cut two
(one reversed)
Fur fabric

F

Paw pad (arm)
Cut two
Brown felt

E

Paw pad (leg)
Cut two
Brown felt

Side head
Cut two
(one reversed)
Fur fabric

Eye

C A

D B

C
A
C

Head gusset
Cut one
Fur fabric

D

D

TIME FOR BED

This hot water bottle cover is a delightful companion for any child to take to bed on a cold winter's night. In summer, the cover could also double as a nightdress case.

You will need:
50cm (½yd) fur fabric
Red, brown and black felt
Black embroidery thread
Polyester filling
1m (1yd) striped cotton fabric
13cm (5in) red cord for hot water bottle
Small square of white cotton fabric
5cm (2in) elastic, 5mm (¼in) wide
Two 1cm (½in) buttons and 1 white pom-pom

To make the cover, draw the pattern on pages 54 and 55 to the full size as described on page 7. Make cardboard templates of the pattern pieces, marking them with an arrow to indicate the direction of pile, and any other relevant information, such as darts and slits.

Lay the templates on to the fabric and draw around them with a felt-tip pen. If two asymmetrical pieces are required, turn the template over before drawing the second one (without changing the direction of pile) to get a mirror image.

Cut out all the pieces with a pair of sharp scissors. Also cut a circle of black felt 6.5cm (2½in) across for the hot water bottle 'stopper', and a strip of red felt measuring 10×1.5cm (4×⅝in). For the handkerchief, you will need a piece of white cotton fabric 15cm (6in) square. Now follow the step-by-step instructions overleaf to make up the bear.

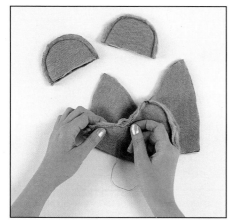

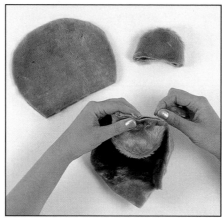

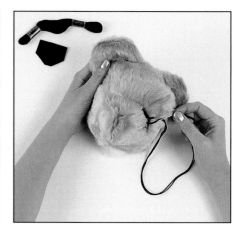

1 Sew the ears together in pairs, leaving the bottom straight edge open. Place the two side head pieces together, with right sides facing, and machine sew along seam A-B. Open the work out and pin the head gusset into place along one side, starting at point A and finishing at C. Sew the gusset to the head, easing the fabric to avoid any tucks. Repeat for the other side.

2 Turn the ears the right way out and machine sew across the bottom edge through both layers. Pin one ear to the head as shown, with all raw edges together. Match the centre of the ear with the seam of the head and gusset. Sew the ear into place. Repeat the procedure with the other ear and then machine sew the back head piece into place, from D to D.

3 Turn the head the right way out and inspect all the seams. Stuff the head and, using double thickness black embroidery thread, embroider the eyes and mouth, referring to the diagram on the page opposite. Turn a small hem all around the black felt nose and, using small stitches, sew the nose into place. Alternatively you can embroider the nose.

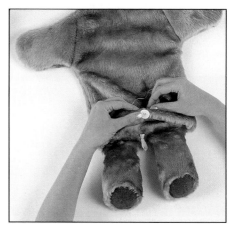

4 Fold the legs in half and sew seam E-F, leaving the top and bottom straight edges open. Open out the base of the feet and sew the felt paw pads into place, pinning and tacking (basting) as usual before machine sewing. Turn the legs the right way out and fill with a little stuffing. Sew across the top of the legs, with the seam centrally placed at the front.

5 Cut the leg slits, as marked, in one of the body pieces. Place the body pieces together with right sides facing and machine sew all around, leaving the bottom straight edge open. Push the ends of the legs through the slits as shown, and sew through all thicknesses. Turn up the section below the legs to form a deep hem and slip stitch in place only at the front.

6 Turn the body the right way out and inspect and brush all the seams. Place a little stuffing in each arm and top-stitch across the arm to the shoulder to keep the filling in place. Fold the elastic in half and sew to the body, between the legs, to form a loop. Sew a button to the other side to match. Using black embroidery thread, embroider claws on each paw.

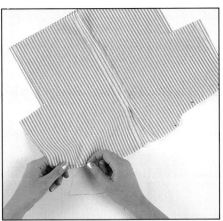

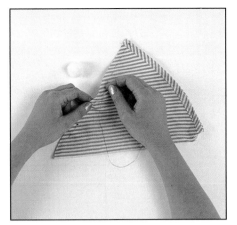

7 *Make a well in the filling inside the bear's head. Place your hand inside the body of the bear and push the neck section into the head, easing it into position. Still keeping one hand inside the neck, sew the head to the body with ladder stitch and strong thread. Continue around the head several times before finishing off firmly.*

8 *Sew the pocket to the front of the shirt. Sew the two front pieces together, leaving an opening at the top. With the front and back pieces together, sew across the shoulders and arms. Hem the sleeve ends, then sew the side seams, leaving an opening at the bottom (which should be top-stitched). Finally, hem the bottom and around the neck.*

9 *Sew a button at the neck of the nightshirt and an elastic loop opposite. Fold the hat in half and sew the dart. Open the hat out and hem the base. Fold the hat in half again, with right sides together, and sew along the side seam. Turn the hat the right way out and sew a pom-pom firmly to the end. Put the hat on the bear and slip stitch in place.*

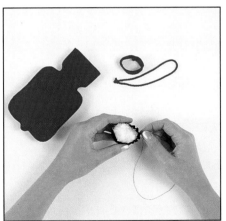

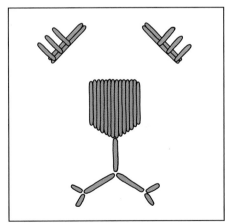

10 *Hem a square of white cotton fabric to make a hanky for the bear's pocket. To make the hot water bottle, draw the bottle shape on to a double layer of red felt and machine sew around the line, leaving the top straight edge open. Using a pair of sharp scissors, cut around the shape close to the stitching. Fill the bottle with a little stuffing.*

11 *Sew a running stitch around the edge of the black circle of felt, put a little filling in the centre and draw the thread tightly. Push this ball into the neck of the bottle and stitch into place. Sew a loop of cord to the neck of the bottle. Stitch the ends of the felt strip together to form a loop and place it around the neck of the bottle; slip stitch in place.*

Use double thickness thread to embroider the face. Push the needle through from the bottom of the head to the inside corner of the eye. Sew a long straight stitch for the eye slit and three small stitches for lashes. Sew the other eye and finish with the mouth. For the nose, either sew a piece of black felt in position or embroider it using satin stitch as here.

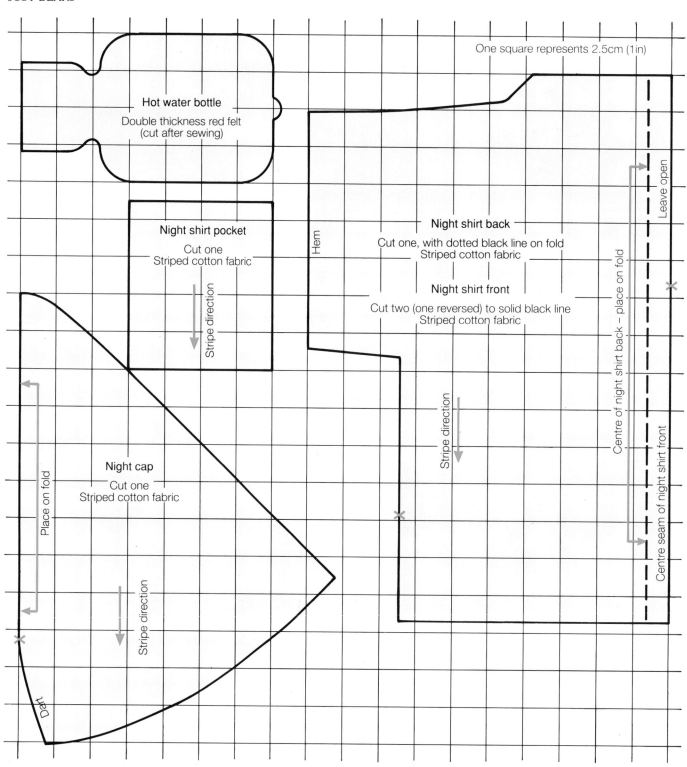

One square represents 2.5cm (1in)

Hot water bottle
Double thickness red felt
(cut after sewing)

Night shirt pocket
Cut one
Striped cotton fabric

Stripe direction

Hem

Night shirt back
Cut one, with dotted black line on fold
Striped cotton fabric

Night shirt front
Cut two (one reversed) to solid black line
Striped cotton fabric

Stripe direction

Leave open

Centre of night shirt back – place on fold

Centre seam of night shirt front

Night cap
Cut one
Striped cotton fabric

Place on fold

Stripe direction

Dart

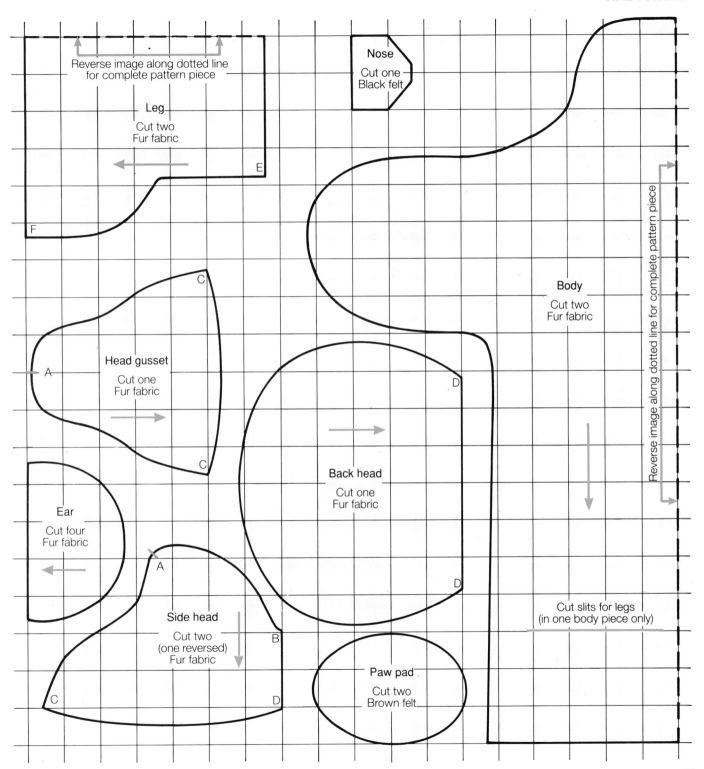

Reverse image along dotted line
for complete pattern piece

Leg
Cut two
Fur fabric

E

F

Nose
Cut one
Black felt

Body
Cut two
Fur fabric

Reverse image along dotted line for complete pattern piece

C

A

Head gusset
Cut one
Fur fabric

C

D

Ear
Cut four
Fur fabric

Back head
Cut one
Fur fabric

A

D

Side head
Cut two
(one reversed)
Fur fabric

B

Cut slits for legs
(in one body piece only)

C

D

Paw pad
Cut two
Brown felt

Clowning Around

This charming clown marionette is designed for children of seven years and over. It will occupy their time for hours, learning how to manipulate the limbs and untie the knots! The outfit would look equally effective made with bold colours in a harlequin design.

You will need:
30cm (⅜yd) fur fabric
16.5mm pair of safety eyes
1m (1yd) thick cord
Small piece of brown felt
Polyester filling
Teasel brush
Black embroidery thread
1m (1yd) striped cotton fabric
1.5m (1½yd) ribbon, 4cm (1½in) wide
Two pieces of wood, one measuring
    2×1×25cm (1×½×10in), the other
    2×1×38cm (1×½×15in)
3 small wooden beads
Thick thread or twine

Enlarge the pattern and prepare cardboard templates. Cut out all the fabric parts, noting the direction of pile. Make up the head as described in step one, page 48, but leave a small gap at the base of the head into which to insert a piece of cord, and a larger gap at the back for turning and stuffing. Then proceed with step one above.

To make the cross bar for step nine, first sand the lengths of wood to ensure there are no splinters. Then glue the two pieces together to form a cross and leave to dry. Drill a small hole in the centre of the crossbar and a hole through each end of the short piece of wood. Drill holes through the side of the long piece.

1 *Cut five 17.5cm (7in) lengths of cord and knot them at both ends. Push the end of one piece through the hole at the base of the head and sew the knot in place. Pierce holes for the eyes, turn the head and insert the safety eyes. Stuff the head firmly and close the gap. Then turn the ears and sew them in place. Finally, embroider the nose referring to page 47.*

2 *Fold the legs in half and pin a knotted cord to the top of each leg, between the two layers of fabric. Machine sew around the leg, leaving a gap for turning and the lower straight edge open. Sew the felt paw pads into place at the base of the legs, easing the fabric carefully. Turn the legs the right way out. Prepare the arms in the same way but without the pads.*

3 *Pierce small holes on the body sides as indicated on the pattern. Push the ends of the arm cords through the arm holes and sew in place on the wrong side of the fabric. Repeat for the legs. Sew the two darts on each body piece. Then place the body pieces together with right sides facing and sew all around leaving a gap in the back seam for turning.*

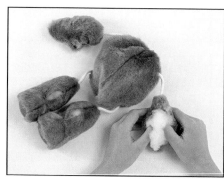

4 *Turn the body the right way out and inspect all the seams. Stuff the arms and legs firmly, and ladder stitch the openings. Stuff the body firmly, keeping the shape nicely rounded, and close the gap with a ladder stitch. Now brush all the seams carefully with a teasel brush, paying particular attention to the areas which have been hand stitched.*

5 *Supporting the head with the left hand, sew the knotted end of the head cord to the top of the body using strong thread. Make quite sure that the head is firmly attached by oversewing a number of times across the cord and finishing off firmly. It is important that the head is firmly joined to the body at this stage as it is a point of stress during play.*

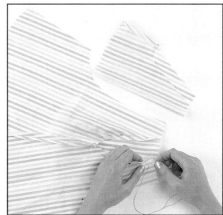

6 *Place the bear to one side and make up the clothing. Sew the side seams E-F on the clown suit. Sew seam E-G on the sleeves; fold the sleeves in half and, with right sides together, sew to the suit, matching points D-E-D. Place the two halves of the suit together, with right sides facing, and sew the centre front and back seams H-J.*

7 *Sew the leg seam K-J-K. Put the suit on the toy and gather the fabric around the legs, arms and neck using running stitch. For the frill, cut a strip of fabric 70×10cm (28×4in) and sew the ends together to form a loop. Fold in half lengthways and sew running stitch along the raw edges. Put the frill around the bear's neck and gather to fit. Repeat with ribbon.*

8 *Fold the hat in half and sew along the straight edge. Turn it the right way out and stuff softly. Gather the base leaving a hole in the centre. Cut a piece of striped fabric 70×10cm (28×4in) to make a frill as described in step seven. Sew the frill to the hat and place over one ear of the bear, sewing it in place using a ladder stitch. Add bows to the hat, chest and ankles.*

9 *Sew a length of twine to the top of the head and push the other end through the hole in the cross centre. Tie a bead to the cord and glue in place. String the feet to the short side bars, ensuring they hang correctly. To finish, attach one end of a length of twine to one paw, pass the other end through the hole at the front of the cross and secure it to the other paw.*

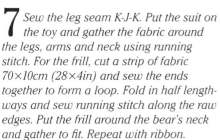

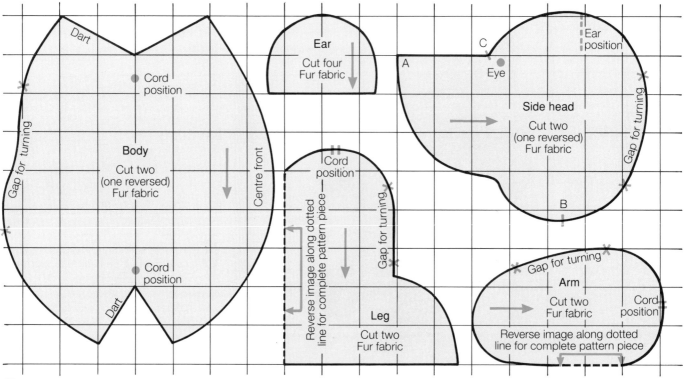

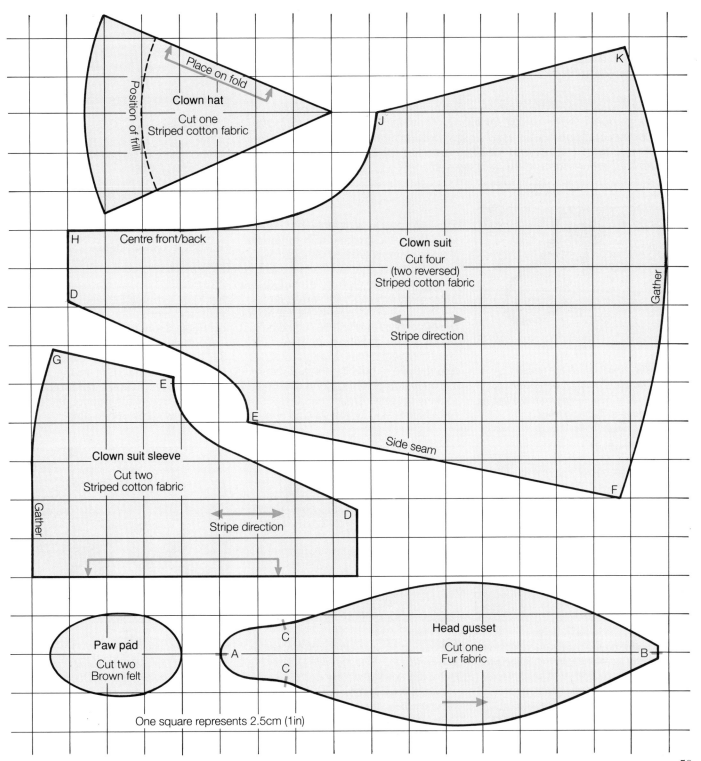

Place on fold

Position of frill

Clown hat
Cut one
Striped cotton fabric

K

J

H   Centre front/back

Clown suit
Cut four
(two reversed)
Striped cotton fabric

Gather

D

⟷
Stripe direction

G

E

E

Side seam

Clown suit sleeve
Cut two
Striped cotton fabric

Gather

⟷
Stripe direction

D

F

Paw pad
Cut two
Brown felt

C

A

C

Head gusset
Cut one
Fur fabric

B

One square represents 2.5cm (1in)

PUPPET SHOW

Your children can create their own puppet shows with these cuddly glove puppets made in soft fur fabric. They are quite simple to make and have special safety eyes and noses, available from craft shops. The puppets will keep babies and toddlers amused for hours, while older children will enjoy making up their own stories.

You will need:
30cm (⅜yd) fur fabric
Small piece of contrasting fur fabric
Polyester filling
13.5mm pair of safety eyes
Small black animal nose
Small piece of striped jersey fabric for scarf
2 pom-poms
Black embroidery thread

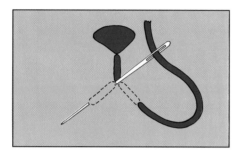

To sew the mouth, push the needle through from the base of the head to the tip of the nose. Sew three small stitches as shown above to form a Y shape.

This is a good project for beginners who wish to start toymaking with fur fabrics. We have simply dressed the bears with a scarf, but you could always make a more complex set of clothes provided you allow plenty of room for movement.

Choose a good quality fur fabric for the puppets as they will be subjected to a lot of strain during play. The fabric should have a certain amount of stretch and the pile should be soft and dense.

You will find some useful tips on toymaking on page 47, so read these carefully before you begin. Always remember to be extremely careful with the use of dressmaker's pins – they can easily be overlooked and not removed.

To make the puppet, first square up the design on page 63, using a 2.5cm (1in) grid and referring to the instructions on page 7. Make cardboard templates of each of the puppet pieces and then follow steps one to nine.

1 *Draw around the cardboard templates on to the back of the fabric, being sure to reverse the side body and head pieces. Cut out the various parts of the puppet. Place the side head pieces right sides together and sew between points A and B. Working from A to C, sew the gusset to one side of the head, and then the other.*

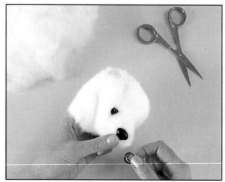

2 *Inspect all the seams carefully before turning the head the right way out. Pierce tiny holes at the eye and nose positions. Insert safety eyes and press the metal washers firmly on to the plastic stalks, inside the head, as far as they will go. Place the nose in positon, also using a safety washer to secure.*

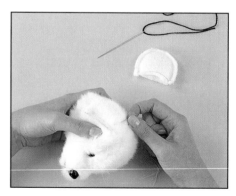

3 *Stuff the head, leaving a space in the centre (for a finger). Using black embroidery thread, sew the mouth according to the diagram. Sew the ears together in pairs, leaving the straight edge open. Turn the right way out and oversew the raw edges. Now sew the ears into position, referring to step four on page 48.*

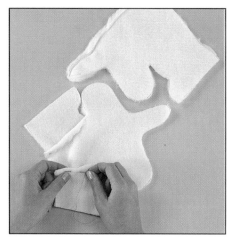

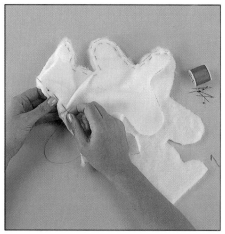

4 *Place the two side body pieces right sides together and machine sew along the seam D-E. Fold the legs inwards, on the front body piece, and sew the darts as indicated on the pattern. Always remember to check that all pins have been removed as they can easily be hidden in the pile of the fur fabric.*

5 *Open out the side body pieces and, with right sides together, lay them in position on top of the front body. Starting at point D, pin, tack (baste) and machine sew around the edge to point F. Repeat on the other side of the body. Then sew the base of the leg on either side between point G and the dart.*

6 *Carefully pin the paw pads to the open foot area, easing the fabric as you go. Tack (baste) the pads into place and then machine sew, making sure there are no tucks of fabric. The paw pads can either be made in a contrasting colour (as here) or in the same colour as the bear if preferred.*

7 *Turn up a small single hem around the bottom edge of the puppet body and pin into place. Using small strong stitches, oversew the raw edge of the hem into place. Knitted fur fabric does not fray so it is not necessary to turn a double hem. After inspecting all seams, turn the body the right way out.*

8 *Place your hand inside the body, with one finger inside the neck section. Push the neck firmly into the puppet head, turning the head a little from side to side for a snug fit. Using strong thread, ladder stitch the head to the body, pulling the thread firmly. Sew around the neck several times in this way before finishing off.*

9 *Cut a piece of jersey fabric 45×10cm (18×4in). Fold in half lengthways then machine sew along the straight edge, leaving both ends open. Turn the scarf the right way out. Turning in the raw edges of the fabric, gather the ends of the scarf with a running stitch. Using strong thread, sew a pom-pom to each end.*

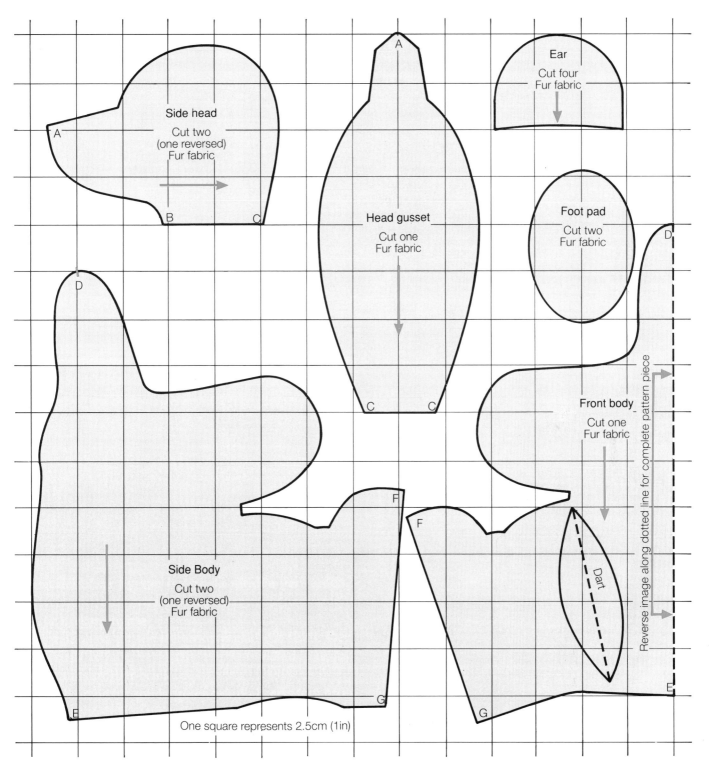

Side head
Cut two
(one reversed)
Fur fabric

A

B   C

Ear
Cut four
Fur fabric

A

Head gusset
Cut one
Fur fabric

C   C

Foot pad
Cut two
Fur fabric

D

Front body
Cut one
Fur fabric

Reverse image along dotted line for complete pattern piece

D

E

D

F

F

Dart

Side Body
Cut two
(one reversed)
Fur fabric

E   G   G

One square represents 2.5cm (1in)

*I*NDEX

ACKNOWLEDGEMENTS

The publishers would like to thank the following
for their help in compiling this book:

Baby Boots Ltd., Nottingham

Mothercare UK Ltd.

Village Pine, London NW1